COVERING THE COURT

COVERING THE COURT

by Edward T. Chase

UNITED STATES TENNIS ASSOCIATION
INSTRUCTIONAL SERIES

Illustrations by George Janes

DOUBLEDAY & COMPANY, INC.
GARDEN CITY, NEW YORK
1976

Library of Congress Cataloging in Publication Data

Chase, Edward Tinsley.
Covering the court.

(Instructional series)
1. Tennis. I. Title. II. Series.
GV995.C43   796.34'22

ISBN: 0-385-05502-1
Library of Congress Catalog Card Number 74–12679
Copyright © 1976 by Edward T. Chase
All Rights Reserved
Printed in the United States of America
First Edition

Contents

COVERING THE COURT

I

Dig You Must

I am going to go to the heart of the matter right here at the outset, to state the crux of the book, which, if put into action, can revolutionize your success at tennis. *The ability to cover the court is the most basic condition for winning in tennis.* Indeed, it is basic for playing the game at all and enjoying it, for tennis is inescapably a running game. (Manuel Orantes' straight-set victory over Jimmy Connors in the 1975 final of the U. S. Open is a dramatic example of this.)

Court coverage is not by any means the exclusive condition for winning. Obviously there is no point in getting to the ball if you don't have the means to make the shot once there. However, among the millions of players below the circuit tournament class, from hackers to local club champions, most matches are won by the player making the fewest errors as opposed to making the more outright placements. So, for most of us, the ability to get in position to make one's shot is decisive. And "hanging in"—that is, getting and then keeping the ball in play—is the *sine qua non* of winning tennis. It is a commonplace that digging, scrambling, getting that ball back, never mind how inelegantly or with how little pace, is crucial, whereas stroking style, for all its aesthetic pleasure and importance, is secondary.

Digging, scrambling, getting that ball back is crucial.

I'll recall a telling example of this. Chris Evert, now a great court coverer—as she has to be, since, not being a natural volleyer, her backcourt ground game even today is still her forte—illustrated the essentiality of "digging" in her famous debut match against Billie Jean King in the nationals at Forest Hills in 1969, where Chris exasperated me and other buffs by her return-of-service action. Yes, Chris would return beautifully, but having hit the ball, she then stood anchored to the spot watching her return, seemingly expecting an outright winner. But Billie Jean is too good a volleyer for that—she'd get her racket on the ball, even on most of the tough returns, and make some kind of first volley. What Chris should have done was *dig* the instant she made her shot—propel herself back toward the center of the court, scramble to get to Billie Jean's first volley the way she does today.

If the server's first volley is not sufficiently lethal, the server is truly vulnerable, especially against so secure a ground stroker as Chris. In that early match, Chris often could have scrambled to the ball and made enough passing shots off Billie Jean's weaker first volleys to break service. But at sixteen she did not automatically dig, did not automatically hit and run or try all out to position herself to keep the ball in play, striving for the eventual opening for the winner. The first axiom of court coverage is to get to the ball and keep it in play.

COURT COVERAGE AND THE DIMENSIONS OF THE COURT

There is a fundamental reason why digging pays off. It has to do with the size and shape of the tennis court. Indeed, a strong case can be made that the genius of tennis as a game is that, by happenstance or brilliant design, the dimensions of the court—for singles seventy-eight feet long, twenty-seven feet wide, net at the center three feet high—are uncannily geared to the human being's physical capacities; that is, the court is exactly the right length and width, the net the proper height, to be beautifully geared to man's natural speed, adroitness, and strength. A significantly smaller or significantly larger court would not permit the fullest expression of man's potential tennis prowess. That is really why there has been no change in the modern court, despite occasional movements to effect one change or another (mostly to de-emphasize the serve). There is a thumb rule in tennis that, if one is in proper position, virtually any shot can be handled, that theoretically there is an "answer" to every shot. "If you can get to it, you can make it."

Now, the corollary of this fact of the ideal dimensions of the game is that the average healthy young person, given basic tennis know-how and decent physical conditioning, can assume a potential ability to cover nine tenths of the shots he will confront.

Court coverage, however, is a sophisticated skill, not an easy skill that any natural athlete can automatically apply to tennis, no matter how fast he or she is. This is so because court coverage must be learned through experience, many hours of tennis playing, facing countless coverage problems. That is where this book can serve its purpose: conveying the distillation of experience and analysis based on years of play and study.

I remember a few years back the world-record sprinter Dave Sime, a born athlete and a fair tennis player, playing at the former New York tennis mecca, the Town Tennis Club, and despite his incredible speed he simply lacked the court-coverage savvy of far slower but experienced players. Or take Pancho Gonzales. The unsophisticated public image of the legendary Pancho has always been of the smasher, the big hitter, and indeed Pancho was that, particularly on his serve and overhead. But his secret weapon—and increasingly in his final decade of competitive play—has been his great coverage, unusual speed, and canniness in getting to every ball with his long reach, discouraging his opponents by returning the ball, and not always very hard (if usually very, very deep).

Watch Pancho's slow, just-over-the-net, slightly underspin deep backhand down the line from out-of-court position and from a defensive stance. This is as indisputably Pancho's trademark as his unsurpassed serve.

Cliff Richey, for another example, has managed to stay fairly near to the world's top among pros (he won forty-seven of his seventy-four matches in a recent typical year, for a 63.5 per cent win percentage) with far less than first-rate stroking equipment; with a forced, unnatural serve; and with a small if muscular physique. Why? Because of his ferocious digging for the ball. He runs down balls less determined if more gifted and faster players never would get to. The same goes for his remarkable sister, diminutive Nancy Richey Gunter, who won thirty-two of forty-six matches a year ago, for a 69.5 per cent win percentage, and who rivals Chris Evert in backcourt tenacity supplemented by a profound knowledge of court-coverage tactics.

Looking at the present and ahead, from our perspective of court coverage, it will be fascinating to watch the evolution of the wave of young new talents already beginning to displace the heroes of old, in particular Jimmy Connors (twenty-two), the former Wimbledon and Forest Hills champion; Bjorn Borg, the twenty-year-old Swedish sensation; lefty Guillermo Vilas, twenty-four, the Argentine star who rose to the top in 1974, with his defeats of Newcombe and Nastase in the Commercial Union Grand Prix tournament in Melbourne, Australia; and possibly Vijay Amritraj, the twenty-year-old Indian Davis Cup star. This is a breathtakingly talented group, and it is interesting to observe that maybe the most brilliantly endowed but least successful of the four so far, Amritraj, is

felt by knowledgeable observers to have the least prom-
ise. Why? Because he is so richly gifted that things come
to him effortlessly, so that he appears under no pressure
to dig. It is all effortless grace. Vilas, Borg, and Connors,
in contrast, are the fiercest of diggers, with Connors running down and pulverizing the ball *off the ground* as no
other player in recent memory, and Vilas and Borg for-
ever converting helpless situations into winning points by
the *élan* of their court coverage and bravura offensive
ground strokes, often while seeming to be *in extremis*.
Dick Stockton and Vitas Gerulaitis may not be far
behind. Manuel Orantes, of course, has already proven his
world-class ranking largely thanks to uncanny court-
coverage ability, and this applies almost equally to Jan
Kodes, the No. 1 Czech, and to Eddie Dibbs and Harold
Solomon.

Few would have predicted several years back, when
serve and volley seemed to be the total answer to winning
tennis—a notion crystallized in the early post-World War
II years by Jack Kramer's concept of "percentage tennis"
—that the rising new stars cited would stand out for the
severity and solidity of their *ground* games, with Connors, in particular, being able in consequence to dominate
his matches by such devastating service returns that he is
able to nullify the big servers time and again.

This is a development of critical importance for the future quality of the game. It is also a matter of vast
gratification to teaching pros and especially to older
players who have made the point to the heedless young
that great tennis necessarily comprises truly solid, effective ground strokes and court coverage, not simply serve
and volley. No champions will prevail in the future with-

out the (once traditional) mastery of the all-court game and its crucial requirement of ground-stroke mastery.

It is only fair to say, of course, that Connors, Borg, and Vilas are fine servers and volleyers, too, *but they would not be at the supreme level they are in world-class play on the merits of their serve and volleying prowess; it is the excelling talents they have in court coverage and ground strokes that have distinguished them from the pack.*

Native talent aside, superior court coverage is a matter of (1) will, (2) shrewd tennis savvy (the ability to anticipate where the ball is going to be returned, and (3) conditioning—each much more decisive than sheer speed afoot. From the long perspective, both in today's game and *historically,* court coverage is *a* if not *the* basic component of winning tennis and is the rationale for this book.

But if court coverage is of consequence for the stars, it is tenfold so for the average player and the beginner and the hacker, since for them it is the elimination of errors, the keeping the ball in play, that is the payoff. The stars do not need to read such a book, needless to say, and any reader who can make the decisive putaway volleys of the world-class stars should not waste time on it. But that eliminates only a tiny fraction of 1 per cent of the world's players. For the rest, who are mostly dependent upon what the Aussies call "groundies," let's move on to specifics.

II

Pre-Match Preparations

Meeting the challenge of court coverage begins as one goes on the court, before play itself. It really does matter that one be dressed for action—that is, shorts or dresses that don't bind and are not of the synthetic material that makes perspiration result in the garment sticking to one and inhibiting movement and concentration. (And once you are fully warmed up, take off any warm-up suit or heavy outer clothes.) Shoes should be as light as is consistent with ruggedness. Some of the new leather ones are surprisingly light, but look out for those that tend to cut the inside of the foot above the instep because of their stiffness. Chafing and blisters are anathema to the court coverer. Appropriately thick sweat socks are *de rigueur*, even the wearing of two pairs if one's feet tend to blister (and if you are playing on cement or asphalt composition). Canvas sneakers remain first-rate gear (and have been improved), and a case can be made for play on hard surfaces for the feeling of security and the long-lasting character of thick-soled sneakers, though they are a bit heavy.

Bearing in mind as you step on the court that you are about to run and stretch, be sure to limber up in the warm-up so as to avoid muscle strains, especially when you are over thirty (sore joints and stiffness are the single

An exercise that will loosen up the tendons in your feet and lower leg.

most important maladies afflicting all tennis players once they are out of their twenties). A good idea, in fact, is to run once or twice around the court on your side of the net and then once from the baseline to the net, building to sprint speed. Embarrassed to look eccentric? It is a small cost for avoiding muscle pulls, or, almost as bad, double faulting in your first service game from stiffness.

And stretch before you play—for example, by leaning out from a wall touched only by your fingertips, an "exercise" that will loosen up the tendons in your feet and lower leg so as to preclude an Achilles tendon tear. This only takes a minute or two but it is good insurance. Remember, *the first game of a set is second in importance only to the final game* (world-class stars also point for the seventh game), so the court coverer makes certain he is loosened up before play starts. Knee bends, though, particularly the old hands-on-the-hips squatting knee bends, are *verboten*. Even pro football players are warned away from that old-hat exercise because it poses unnecessary risk to knee cartilage, the single biggest incapacitator in active sports.

It goes almost without saying that one must assume good general conditioning if one is to excel at court coverage and this means beyond anything else *running* power. The best conditioner is to play an hour or more of singles daily. But few of us can arrange this so my recommendation is to get in fifteen minutes of jogging, no more, no less, every other day. Before dinner at the end of the workday is a good time. This does wonders for your wind, legs, a more efficient metabolism, and your morale. You simply feel much better for it.

Do practice serves and overheads in the warm-up, not so much to groove the stroke but to loosen back, shoulder, and hip muscles. A good tactic here is to *start* each warm-up rally with a serve instead of just hitting the ball from your hand. This provides just the minimum loosening up of those serving muscles desirable before play begins. This does not take the place of your actual practice serves (but it minimizes their need and by so doing it means your opponent has less chance to familiarize himself with your serve, an initial advantage for you). Take the regular practice serves too, unless you're playing for fun, first ball in, the weekend hacker's psychological crutch shot and a bad habit.

So now you are about to play a set or two, or a match. Since covering the court effectively is an act of *will* as much as it is a technical feat, *one's attitude at the start of play is worth attention.* In fact, this is a matter almost universally overlooked, and yet its importance can hardly be overstated—at least for the court coverer. The key personal injunction to give yourself is to remember this: Any time you are playing sets and games—that is, keeping score—*you are playing a match.* O.K., so it's not a tournament (though sometimes it's that), but it is always a match. The point here is that your attitude going on the court must be "I'm into a match, I want to win it, I intend to dig for every ball," for the truth is that no one especially enjoys having *lost* a match, no matter how friendly it was, *after* the event. This is particularly true, as is so often the case, when it is either a contest with an opponent or opponents you may not get a crack at again ever, or for some time—hence to chance to redeem yourself—or is a contest with your regular opponent in a continuing series that you *do* care about, or you wouldn't bother to continue it. So actually say silently to yourself, "Every match is a match"; don't flub it; play it well—or else you'll regret it later for having messed up a good game (also somewhat spoiled it for your opponent and, if doubles, for your partner).

Now, this attitude is especially decisive for the court coverer, who accepts very consciously the basic challenge of keeping the ball in play.

Is all this too grim for just a game? Not at all. The truly deadly thing in tennis isn't caring; it is *not* caring, trivializing the game by failing to put anything consistent into it, the "What's the difference?" attitude of kids who carelessly bash balls around the court. It isn't tennis, and, for those over ten, it isn't fun.

III

Match Play

O.K., you're going into a match, warmed up, determined, ready to go. We have been discussing pre-match physical (the warm-up) and psychological (the attitude) fundamentals for the court coverer. Pursuing this theme, as we begin the game, the next point to stress is *what is the most effective method of starting a match*. This is highly important, especially for the many romantics among us who think they can pull off a Borg or a Rosewall—that is, come from way behind after a bad start, just by wishing it.

Two or three basic factors merit emphasis. First, unless you are an Arthur Ashe—and you aren't—do not begin with an all-out effort in the sense of trying for outright spectacular winners, going into highest gear at the outset. A surprising number of players, particularly young ones, will try this, figuring that they have to start grooving their big shots right off. They are impatient to hit out, without restraint, from the opening gong.

Now, it *is* psychologically easier to do this. One has a sense of relief. But percentagewise, it is a poor tactic, and the consequences can turn the whole match spiraling toward defeat.

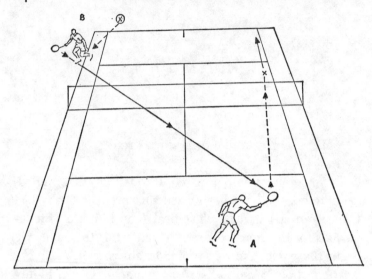

Hitting the logical shot: Player A has pulled Player B wide offcourt. B manages a defensive shot back to A, who hits safely to the logical open area, a short, easy shot at maximum distance from B and one easy for A to execute.

Remember, in the court coverer's system, the primary concern has to be minimization of errors. As the errors *necessarily* mount up when one goes for broke on each shot at the outset, then self-assurance fades, the opponent's self-assurance grows, and desperation tactics may take over. An important footnote to this: As you gain experience, you will be comforted by the observation of something veteran players already know—hurricanes blow out; if by chance your opponent does manage to blow you off the court at the very outset, you need not panic be-

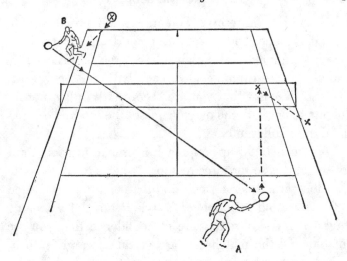

Hitting the wrong shot: Player A needlessly risks a too difficult drop shot, which is netted, when the opponent B is
clearly out of contention. Thoughtless players frequently make
this error in judgment.

cause it is axiomatic that the cycle will presently end and
the hot hand will turn cold.

In any event, the proper approach is to try to start a
match well within oneself. That does not mean play ten-
tatively or tightly, but rather with sufficient pace and
depth to prevail, without *excessive* pace. It also means
hitting the *logical* shot (that is, the shot to the open
court, not the too-clever, second-guess shot that is spectacular). In short, *build up to a faster pace and to in-
creased pressure on the opponent*. You have, thereby,

held something in reserve. You are steadily progressing to a tougher game. You are covering court assiduously from the outset, giving nothing away easily, no unearned, silly errors. You are running down each ball and seeing to it first and foremost that you are keeping it in play, not indulging in overkill, the overhit smash, the too, too complicated drop volley, etc.

Now, this "build up" approach is crucial to good court coverage. It is so for three reasons: It helps to compensate for one's natural nervousness and the need to get oriented to the court and the opponent's style in a match's opening stages; it fortifies your sense of confidence that you are not blowing the match and are getting securely into it; and playing within yourself at the start saves precious energy.

As experience will reveal, often a player will find himself winded, curiously out of breath very early in a match —an alarming development for all us court coverers. But don't be alarmed. This is purely the physiological effect of early-match nervous anxiety, and presently one's wind returns. Indeed, if the match is a long one, you will even get a genuine second wind, so-called, that bonus effect of greater lung power that is quite common if you're in good running condition.

REALITIES OF PLAY

Now let us come to grips with the actual tactical realities of match play and the philosophy behind the key shots.

At all levels of play, from hacker to world class, the

serve, first, and return of service, second, are *the* crucial shots in the game even on the slowest clay surfaces. No one can play winning tennis when his or her serve is "off"—one's whole game deteriorates, psychologically as well as structurally. So we shall confront the serve and its return first of all. What has service to do with court coverage? A great deal. It is an integral part of it because court coverage means *keeping the ball in play*, and the serve, the only self-initiated shot, is *the most important in the chain of shots comprising a rally or a point.*

From the viewpoint of this book—that is, court coverage—the service is not only a prime offensive weapon, it must also be hit (a) so as to be free of error and (b) to enhance the server's effective court coverage, in order to reduce the server's vulnerability to service returns that are impossible to cover.

Obviously the happiest course would be to serve ace after ace, or such powerful serves as to elicit immediate error. But this is a book for mortals, not magicians or world-class players. So the first reasonable requisite is consistency rather than power per se. Adopt the psychology that getting one's *first* serve in four out of five or five out of six times is the standard you'll demand of yourself. Technique is of vast importance in this regard. But getting one's first serve in requires above all else concentration and willpower.

If there is a single basic point to stress regarding this matter of consistency of service it is this: Whatever the particular style of your service—a book on court coverage won't attempt to teach the specific serve actions—see that it is *simple*, that is, not a compound of complicated motions that thereby increase the chances for faulty execu-

It is axiomatic that the more complex the function, the greater the risk of mistake. Unless you are by luck a natural big server, it is better to mimic the simple service action of a Ken Rosewall or a Billy Talbert than to try the great but more complicated action of a Fred Stolle or a Neale Fraser.

tion. It is axiomatic that the more complex the function (any function), the greater the risk of mistake. Better to mimic the simple service action of a Ken Rosewall or a Billy Talbert than to try the great but more complicated action of, say, a Fred Stolle or a Neale Fraser.

The toss is at the heart of service consistency. This must be an intensely conscious, thought-through movement that is grooved, unwavering, if one is to attain a high percentage of first serves in. Almost equally important, be careful of footwork, something generally overlooked when it comes to serving. Next to the inconsistent, bad toss, the biggest error in service technique is in sloppy footwork, especially in bringing the back foot forward too soon. Be balanced and set, not hopping or wavering in your stance. And the third most important factor is keeping your eye on the ball—seeing to it the ball is hit dead center in your strings. Yes, on the service, too, this is critically important.

Next, practice grooving the serve to cut into the "T" in the deuce court, and the backhand corner in the ad court (reverse against lefties). Sure, there will be exceptions; but most opponents will have more trouble dealing with the serve on their extended backhand corner than on the forehand. (It goes without saying that you must occasionally alternate hitting to the forehand both to pick up a stray point through surprise and to keep the opponent "honest": not running around your serve to take it on his forehand.) You *always* serve to a target spot. You may not hit it, but the very effort of focusing on it acts to discipline the shot and enhance consistency.

The good court coverer in singles will stand to serve pretty close to the center of his baseline to afford maxi-

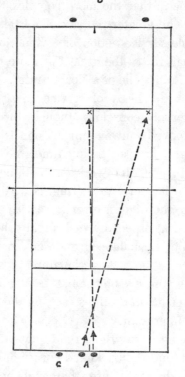

Serving: A   Positions for serving in ad and deuce courts.
        B   Receiver positions
        C   Wrong serving position

Practice grooving the serve to cut into the "T" in the deuce court (that is, the opponent's extended backhand corner) and into the backhand corner in the ad court (reverse against lefties).

Note on same diagram, the good court coverer in singles will stand to serve pretty close to the center of his baseline to afford best access to any returns, to protect against, for instance, a backhand return down the forehand line, dangerous if he's serving from the ad court from too far over toward his own backhand corner.

mum access to any returns, to protect against, say, a backhand return down his forehand line, dangerous if he's
serving from the ad court from too far over toward his
own backhand corner.

It is difficult to overstate the advantages to a court
coverer of club-play level of placing his *first* serve in, not
having to depend on his second serve. This is so almost
more for psychological reasons than for any other. On the
one hand, getting one's first serve in consistently im-
mensely bolsters your confidence; on the other hand, it
precludes the receiver from zeroing in and exploiting the
generally weaker and more easily gaugeable second serve.
It is an immense advantage for the court coverer; he has
preserved himself from being put *in extremis;* he is con-
trolling the play. And to hold service is a major morale
booster. The only all-time great to retire undefeated in
head-to-head pro tour play, Jack Kramer, did it by virtue
of a great forehand, but even more because he got his first
service in, and if not, got in the toughest second serve in
the game's history.

With respect to the serve, the court coverer must study
his opponent in the first instance to minimize "getting
hurt" by the return. For example, it may be that your opponent is disconcertingly steady and consistent in returning your serves to his backhand, so you are tempted to
serve to his forehand (or vice versa). But the paramount
principle is to avoid setting up a situation with your serve
where you run the danger of losing the point outright or
losing your offensive advantage. Thus, in this instance,
the opponent may have a less *consistent* forehand but a
dangerous one, since when he does get a crack at it, he
puts you in real trouble. Since, as a court coverer, you are

The good court coverer in singles will stand to serve pretty close to the center of his baseline to afford best access to any returns.

bent on keeping the ball in play, it is therefore preferable to serve to that unfailing but less dangerous backhand than to risk the point by exposure to an overpowering forehand return. This, of course, is in keeping with the principle of percentage tennis.

If service is the most important shot, return of service is a close second. The superior court coverer has to be a veritable scholar of service returning, has to master the art. *The rhythm of any tennis match is established by serve and return of serve. Remember these key initiating shots create the structure of the ensuing rally for the point.* Obviously, the point is over pronto if one returns serve, say, with a weak, high shot to the forehand, putting oneself in mortal jeopardy of either a pulverizing first volley if the server comes in or an equally pulverizing forehand drive. No, the court coverer's whole strategy is to *nullify* the server's advantage and to try, best of all, to take over the offensive with one's return or, at the minimum, at least to get the ball *safely* into play.

It is hard to generalize about how to accomplish such a service return because it depends upon the individual character of the server. The best course here is to analyze the various basic situations the returner faces, always bearing in mind that it is the court coverer's viewpoint we are emphasizing.

The first question is the receiver position and how to hold the racket for return. I would urge that the racket be held in essentially the forehand grip (since most players nowadays use the standard eastern "shake hands" grip, this does not mean more than a minute fraction of a shift in the grip anyhow). The reason is that speed of racket work (getting it back and then through) is critical in re-

Receiver position for return of service.

turning a fast serve. By the nature of the human body, it is a longer, more complex action to bring the racket back on the forehand than on the backhand—the latter is simply a direct move of the racket head back across the body.

The ready position for service returns is to lean forward raised on the balls of your feet, with the racket pointed straight ahead in front, lightly cradled or touched by the left hand, midway, so to speak, for either forehand or backhand action, with the receiver ready to hop into action just as the serve is struck so that his body is mobile, already on the move, racket instantly drawn back.

That little jump step or hop sounds odd, perhaps. But if you don't already do it, take a look at the better players and all the circuit tournament players. You'll see how it's done, a fraction of a second before the ball crosses the net, a small move, a hop, that is curiously effective in readying the receiver for returning the serve.

There is an ancient saying that the best defense is a good offense, and *this is particularly true for the court coverer in returning service*. Let's review the basic variations. In each case we are trying to convert the shot into a situation where the offensive is taken over from the server. This means that on the average, if at all possible, aim on hitting a low, hard, deep return to the server who is not following his serve to the net. The objective is an offensive shot hopefully forcing a weak, short, or high return. From a percentage standpoint, generally try to force to the backhand. (Obviously this makes no sense if the server happens to be notably weak on the forehand and strong on the backhand. You then reverse it.)

Still confining the discussion here to the server who is not coming in, an obvious variation to the return is a drop shot, especially on a weak second serve and on a slow clay surface. This strategy introduces an exasperating uncertainty factor the server must confront—assuming you have

The little jump step or hop just as the serve is struck.

the stroking ability to make a drop shot, one that just clears the net and, ideally, has backspin.

If you have the strokes to hit high-bounding serves (most players are more comfortable with low bounds), you may be able to exploit the angles on a high-bounding serve. In his autobiography (with Peter Rowley), Ken

Rosewall remarks how he was able to hit down into extreme angles (instead of deep) on Vic Seixas' characteristically high-bounding serve, one of the reasons Rosewall was Seixas' nemesis from the moment Rosewall entered the world tournament circuit.

Again, while the first requisite above all is to get the ball in play, as a general principle, try to take the returns as close in to the net as you can, *commensurate with the prime necessity of safety of return*. This can mean taking the second serve as many as two to three feet inside the baseline and with the ball slightly on the rise. The advantage of so doing is to put maximum pressure on the server —the return is shooting back to him so he is rushed in his shotmaking and getting into position.

This principle of taking the return as close in as possible of course is doubly important in returning the serve of the player who follows his serve in. You are forcing him thereby to make that crucial shot, the first volley, at his maximum distance from the net, thereby robbing him of the angle advantage he'd have closer to the net, and also forcing him to take a relatively lower, dipping ball that he will have to volley up.

But quite possibly this server who does follow his serve in is hitting too fast and too tough a serve for you to take it in close. As stated above, the *sine qua non* is to get the ball in play, so if it is necessary, return from a foot or two or three behind the baseline, concentrating above all on keeping your return *low, low, low,* forcing the volleyer to hit up or at least denying him the easy smash. Here spin becomes important—a topspin that makes the ball drop, or a chip-shot return with a backspin so as to present a ball that is low, spinning, and offers no pace.

Return of service: By taking the serve as close in toward the
net as is feasible, you are forcing the server who follows his
serve in to make the crucial first volley at his maximum distance from the net, thereby robbing him of the angle advantage he'd have closer to the net and also forcing him to take
a relatively lower, dipping ball that he will have to volley up,
as illustrated here.

The court coverer's dearest wish may now be realized: a weak first volley, the most delicious reward for the court coverer, for, by definition, with his indefatigable focus on coverage, he will get to that first volley and then pass the server, vulnerable at the net, unable to retreat, exposed to a pass or, if the receiver has the time to execute it precisely, a topspin offensive lob over his head and unrecoverable.

The court coverer on service returns axiomatically digs the moment he hits, back into the center court if he has been pulled aside, or pell-mell to wherever the first volley is headed from a server coming in. His supreme obligation is to keep the ball in play, hopefully turning the rally around so that he takes over the offensive from the server, who normally would have the offensive advantage.

An important tip against servers who follow their serves in is this: If the serve is hard and fast or difficult to handle because of spin, the court coverer's best-percentage shot is to concentrate returning low and hard *to the center of the net*. The center, yes. There are several reasons for this. First, because you are endeavoring to hit the lowest possible ball, it is well to hit for the center since the net is appreciably lower there, meaning that even a viciously hard return of service will stay in court and not go long, since its clearance height is so low. The second argument for hitting for the center is that, on a purely geometric basis, if you have partly mishit or mistimed the return because the serve is so hard, the odds are better that if you try to aim for the center, your return is at least hit safely into court—even if you've hit, say, eight or ten feet aside of the desired center. Third, concen-

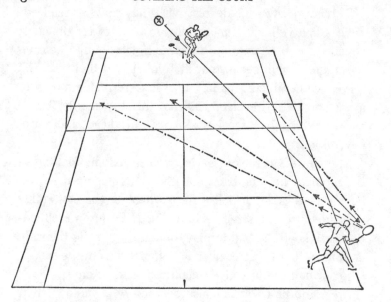

The principle here is to concentrate on returning the service low and hard to the *center of the net area* when you are dealing with a dangerously tough serve, one that may be very fast or pull you wide or has "devil" in its spin. The reasons: On a purely geometric basis, if you have partly mishit or mistimed the return, the odds are that even if you're off some eight or ten feet, by focusing on the center you'll at least get the ball into play. Again, even a hard return at the center won't go long since the net is lowest there, so your clearance height can be low. Save the down-the-line return or the sharply angled return for easier serves that you can handle safely.

trating on the center shot sets up the prospect of more surprise when you do attempt a return either down the line, or a sharply angled crosscourt shot or even a lob—

assuming now that the serve is not quite so lethal and therefore you have the prospect of successfully making these shots. Remember, you are a court coverer, and your guiding principle is to create the situation whereby your strategy, keeping the ball in play, can be best realized.

Yes, a lob—on occasion use it against the serving net rusher, especially if you have pulled wide out of court by his serve. Some of you will recall the famous Forest Hills finals in which Rafael Osuna, the marvelously fast and clever Mexican Davis Cupper, returned the huge serves of Frank Froehling standing some six to eight feet behind the court, putting up lobs forty feet high. This was an extreme instance, but there is a lesson here of what one may be forced to do *in extremis* to keep in the game, to be true to that first axiom of court coverage: *Get the ball into play somehow.*

We are focusing our discussion here on what was noted above to be *the* crucial shots in each point, namely service and return of service, the fact being, as stated earlier, that these shots tend to establish the pattern of play with each point. This principle is of utmost consequence for effective court coverage. Once the rally has begun—that is, serve and return have been accomplished—then the pattern of play on that point is being established. And here some tips are in order.

Note that *each shot tends to produce a like shot in return*—for example, a crosscourt backhand will tend to elicit a crosscourt backhand return; and ditto on the forehand or down-the-line shots. Therefore, if your strength happens to be, say, deep crosscourt backhand, it behooves you to try to create such an exchange. The principle here is to try to create the pattern of play that goes

with *your* strength and *your* best pattern so far as consistent court coverage is concerned.

Now, obviously this is not an absolute principle; for example, taking this example of your best shot being a crosscourt backhand, if your opponent should happen to be a lefty with a potent forehand, you then must weigh your strength against his strength—and you may well conclude that you must hit instead to his weaker backhand side, even though in this instance it is forcing you to adopt a pattern—your forehand crosscourt—that you would normally avoid.

In short, be alert to the pattern you are setting up; carefully measure strengths versus opponents' strengths vis-à-vis patterns of play, *observing that a given shot tends to produce the same shot in kind.* As the match progresses, your analysis of which patterns come out most favorably for you must be the guiding factor in your tactical decisions.

Now to another point. Above we discussed return of service from the viewpoint of the returner who is staying back on his return, hitting against a server coming into the net. This is the most conventional, standard pattern. But, especially among club players and below, many, indeed most, servers will not follow service in, and there then arises the prospect for the aggressive court coverer to exploit his superior service return by going to the net himself. Indeed, this may well be the most appropriate tactic for effective court coverage against a relatively weak serve. Certainly, if one can "tee off" on the weak serve, it follows that a weak, short reply will follow from your strong service return, and it behooves the court coverer to end the point then and there by seizing the

offensive advantage and ending the point with an angled or deep volley rather than allowing this weak server to "get off the hook" and possibly regain the initiative in a subsequent long rally. So a quick *coup de grâce* at the net is also seen to be a proper tactic in the arsenal of the "percentage"-playing court coverer.

Earlier, mention was made of the point that in returning service under severe pressure, the receiver should aim for a low shot to the *center* of the court. This is, in a way, a "center-court theory." But the classic use of that term, of course, is in doubles play, where there are several reasons to play the ball down the center (principally since it both reduces the angle of the subsequent volley and it can effectively create a hesitation and mistiming by the opposing team uncertain as to which player is to play the ball). For the court coverer in singles, the chief attraction of the down-the-center shot is that—apart from the argument introduced earlier—the center shot may effectively modify the opponent's ability to exploit the angles or to enjoy to the fullest his favorite attacking ground stroke. This is so because one must run around, one way or another, a shot down the center deep to the baseline (remember, it *has* to be deep or you're dead), and the hitter does have a much more restricted potential angle. So this deep, down-the-center shot is important for the court coverer's repertoire *since it acts to reduce his exposure to sharply angled shots, including punishing deep shots to the corners.*

IV

Faking and Spin:
Two Potent Tactical Weapons

Effective court coverage has to include tactics designed to limit or nullify the opponent's offensive opportunities. Faking is a relatively sophisticated tactic the beginner cannot expect to use, but for intermediate players and good club players (not to mention circuit players) it is an essential expertise. Faking (or conning the opponent) means persuading or forcing your opponent to hit into a desired area. Here are the two most obvious situations in which this will arise; each of critical concern to court coverage.

1. The first instance is in the case of your having to put up a defensive lob under severe pressure. Let's say the pressure was so severe you ended up popping a weak lob to your opponent's forehand side—a lob too short, too low to give you any real security—and you are trapped off in the backhand position of the court. Now, the curious reality is that, on the statistical average, a good club player will tend to hit his overhead straight down into the backhand corner, so your best bet is to fake a move to cover the open forehand side of your court, but in fact to hold your ground in the backhand court—that's where his smash is most likely to come. A tyro (*or* a really good

1923887

If you are trapped off in the backhand position of the court after being forced to pop up a weak lob to your opponent's forehand side, *fake* a move to cover your own open forehand side of the court *but hold your ground* in the backhand court, as illustrated. The curious reality is that, on the statistical average, a good club player will tend to hit his overhead straight down into your backhand corner. You have a fighting chance to return it.

player) will hit for the open forehand court; if he's a tyro, it will likely be a weak shot, so dig to get it. If he's a top player, just try to take a stab at it. Sometimes you'll be lucky; and the mere fact of your digging maintains a psychological pressure on *any* opponent.

2. Although faking so as to impel your opponent to hit into a desired area is one form of faking that the court coverer needs to cultivate, a second form is the faking you yourself perpetrate in making your shot. For instance, on any *short* ball (near or inside the service line) you have the option of striking the ball hard and deep and following into the net, or faking such a shot as you move in, but instead of smacking it deep to the corner, *arrest the stroke midway, and undercut it for reverse spin for a drop shot that dies.* The opponent, expecting a deep drive and on his heels, so to speak, is caught flat-footed. (And if he has anticipated and starts to move in early, simply hit out deep at the last second and he's dead.) Incidentally, if your opponent manages to get to your drop shot O.K., you are in trouble, especially if you are in fairly close to the net, so you must fake moving fast to cover the biggest open area, with the real intent of conning him into hitting the ball where you can get to it.

More important than fakes for the court coverer is the use of spin, because control is critically important for the court coverer and spin is even more important as an element in control than as an offensive weapon, though it can also be the latter. All strokes can benefit from spin for the sake of control. An Ellsworth Vines may be able to hit flat with abandon, and thereby blow his opponent off the court. But it is a hopeless style percentagewise without his genius. Any properly hit serve will have spin, and it is a good idea to emphasize this spin if you're a court coverer, in singles or doubles—in singles to be certain you get the high percentage of first balls in; in doubles for the same reason but also to enable you to move rapidly into the net before the opponent has had the chance to return

On any short ball you have the option of hitting deep and following in, or (as illustrated) arresting the stroke midway and undercutting for a reverse spin, for a drop shot that dies. With proper concentration these are the club player's bread-and-butter, sure-point-winner shots.

your serve—it arcs in, spinning, giving you those precious additional fractions of a second to run in closer to the net for your first volley.

Heavily undercut spin on the backhand is not an excessively difficult achievement for an intermediate player

and especially for the court coverer it is well worth
developing for occasional deep shots to the corner or a
short down-the-line shot to your opponent's forehand.
The backspin will precipitate errors, with your opponent
liable to underestimate the need to counteract spin.
Hence he flubs the shot—that is, he hits a weak return into
the net, or, in a too-hard shot, he hits way past the baseline, owing to the backspin, which will loft the ball long
when a strong countering topspin has been put on the
ball. On the down-the-line shot also exert a sidespin,
making the ball curve out and die on the alley. Jack
Kramer invariably used this sidespin in his down-the-line
forehand approach shot.

Again, this severe underspin can often wreak havoc on
a volleyer: The spin will often deflect the ball down
sufficiently to go into the net. The court coverer has saved
himself from having to make another second effort!

Conversely, occasional *heavily* topspinning balls hit off
the ground (generally more readily accomplished on the
forehand than the backhand by the average player) will
serve as a "rescue" shot for the court coverer under severe
pressure. For instance, if you are pulled offcourt with
your opponent camped for the kill at the net, one option
(the other is always the lob) is to powder the ball with
the heaviest, dipping topspin you can muster. This does
two things for the court coverer: the topped ball will dip
rapidly below the net forcing an "up" volley, which is
likely to fly high and deep, perhaps over the baseline for
an outright error, or else result in a return volley in a tra-
jectory so high and deep that the court coverer can
scramble to the ball and be back in the play, now able to

have the time and position possibly to pass the net man or
lob him deep. (When Vilas beat John Newcombe in Melbourne for his first great win on grass, he prevailed in part
with this tactic, employing in his case a thunderous
topspin backhand directly at Newcombe.)

The above use of topspin is to convert a defensive position of danger into a saving and winning position, a tactic
in *court coverage* since it contributes to the court coverer's primary task—digging to keep the ball in play. A
comparable expedient, using a shot of very pronounced
topspin in order to break out of a dangerous driving backcourt duel, is to introduce a high topspin lob or semilob
deep to the opponent's backhand. This is not always as
easy as it sounds. But the court coverer may find percentagewise that it is preferable as a means of ending a haz-
ardous (since error-prone) driving duel because such a
high-bounding topspin shot to your opponent's backhand
confronts him with a shot that is virtually impossible to
drive offensively, and it is even more effective if repeated
in sequence. The opponent may flub it if he's at all care-
less or has hit a setup, and you can move on for a putaway. In short, it is (a) a defensive ploy for the court
coverer and (b) a shot that can often be converted into a
winning situation.

How, conversely, should the court coverer handle this
high-bounding topspin lob to his own backhand (one of
the favorite shots, by the way, of one of the East's better
club players, Stanley Rumbough, Jr., active at East
Hampton and Palm Beach)? Two expedients are availa-
ble: The best and most decisive if you have fast enough
reactions is to move in swiftly the instant you see the lob

in the making and take it on a high volley overhead if possible, smashing it away. In short, nullify the shot by *never letting it bounce*. The court coverer has another expedient: Instantly drop back deep so as to take the ball on your backhand at the end of its bounce, so it is hit at orthodox, waist-high level, and hit it on a line drive down the opponent's *forehand* line deep—not crosscourt (down the line because your opponent has hit from his own

Under severe pressure (for instance, if you are pulled way offcourt with your opponent camped for the kill at the net), one option (the other is to lob) is to powder the ball with the heaviest, dipping topspin you can muster (see illustrations "off both wings").

If you are confronted with a high-bounding topspin lob to
your backhand while on the baseline area, and can't move in
to take it overhead, instantly drop back so as to take the ball
on your backhand at the end of the bounce, thus hitting at
orthodox waist-high level (see illustration), and hit it on a
line drive down the line. Only aces can half-volley this shot,
so you must drop back.

backhand corner and thus must be on the run to cover your shot; also, because the down-the-line shot has a shorter distance to go to the baseline and so the ball is that fraction of a second less briefly in play for your opponent to reach it). But it is crucial to bear in mind the risk involved in this shot, namely the greater height of the net on the end and the shortness of distance to the baseline.

This takes us to a point of some consequence to the court coverer: the significance of playing the diagonals in tennis. Here again the objective is to make proper use of the court in the interest of keeping the ball in play, that *sine qua non* of the court coverer. The point is that you gain a differential of some five feet hitting crosscourt to the corners—in short, you gain a substantial leeway, an added margin of court to hit in over the down-the-line shot. This is worth knowing when you are under heavy pressure from an opponent who is getting you in trouble in backcourt. Under pressure, hit the diagonal shot instead of down the line (with the exception noted above), since an imperfectly hit shot will stay in, thanks to the greater margin for error.

Returning briefly to our subject of spin, the court coverer will confront it in its most difficult manifestation when playing left-handed opponents. This is a vexing task for most of us anyhow, since it means facing a reversal of normal patterns, hard to adjust to—the serve spins in to you on the backhand; your favorite forehand drive into the ad court corner dismayingly plays to most lefties' strength, their forehands, etc. Fortunately, most lefties have an exploitable weakness, namely a too sharply undercut backhand. They tend to "wrist" it, undercut it excessively, and are prone to error if forced there. But beware: The ball they hit off their backhand is often quite viciously undercut, with a spin into your forehand that must be very carefully nullified. This is done, above all, first by concentrating on taking the ball in the absolute center of your racket—just a little off and with the heavy spin you'll make an error. Second, you must *hit through* the spin; a simple block will be vulnerable to the spin, and the ball will go awry. Try to topspin it back cross-court to the lefty's backhand (you have a better than fifty-fifty chance of winning that duel of forehand to backhand); *or* slice it (an undercut spin plus sidespin) straight down the line low to his forehand.

Don't try to drop-shot a heavily spinning ball from a lefty's backhand; it requires a master's touch.

If you have speed afoot (you should, as a court coverer) and a decent volley, when you engage a lefty in a crosscourt exchange your forehand to his backhand, attack to the net if possible on the second or third shot, volleying deep to his ad court corner.

When playing the lefty's big weapon, his topspin fore-hand crosscourt drive, the court coverer has to extract himself from this pattern as quickly as possible by hitting the ball down the line to the lefty's backhand, and, *above all else*, if you must hit back to the lefty's forehand, take the chance of hitting as deep as possible. Depth is deci-sive here; a short shot near the service line is tantamount to losing the point with a good club lefty, whose meat-and-potatoes shot is more often than not the short shot on his forehand side. Most lefties can also slice them down your forehand line, as well as pulverize them using topspin to your backhand. So the court coverer must be on the alert to run over to counter that contingency. Yes, court coverage is made extra difficult by the unorthodoxy of lefties' play.

V

Playing to the Score

The court coverer, more so than the serve-volley-smasher, must develop a sense of his "position" with respect to the score in a match, both the pattern of key points within given games *and* also games within the set. Since the court coverer is pledged to sustain the ball in play, to win the all-important battle of attrition (a battle that is as psychological as it is physical), one cannot overstress the advantage of winning the first and second points, in that order. Sounds obvious, doesn't it? Well, the fact is that very few players (except touring pros) give sufficient thought to playing to score. *The psychological lift that comes from winning the first point is almost worth an additional point in itself.* It relieves pressure. The cardinal objective, however, is to get thirty points, ideally thirty–love, but even thirty–fifteen will do. Run yourself ragged to get those precious thirty points, because behold the opportunity you have now created: By winning just one more point at thirty–love, you have the beautiful prospect of three relaxed shots for the game! You now can *afford* to gamble on a real offensive shot once you have reached the thirty-point "no choke" haven—and be even more tension-free and dangerous in your shotmaking if you make that next point (for forty–love). Concentrate, then, for all you're worth *on those first two points*, resolving, as the court coverer you are, not to forgo such a sweet posture of security that thirty points affords by any unforced, hence needless, errors. Court-covering percentage tennis means self-aware, heads-up tennis, not smash and the hell with it. Go for thirty!

The truth of this philosophy is agonizingly apparent if you face the *reverse* situation. Nothing is more demoralizing or tension-creating than to be fighting uphill in your game scores, constantly losing that vital first and then second point. It gives one "the elbow," as they say, creating the choked-up syndrome. Court coverers can't afford that because they accumulate their points methodically, not in a burst.

Further comments about playing to the score: A court coverer in trouble, say down fifteen–forty, by definition will rely *on getting to the ball* to extricate himself, rather than gamble on an all-out winning shot—in short, the exact reverse of being *ahead* forty–fifteen, when a gamble is quite in order. Never try a delicate drop shot or an exotic drive for the chalk when down at game point. Work your way back into the game first!

Now, that does not mean you choke in confronting an intimidating score. Rather it means you reduce gambles. And as a court coverer you cannot afford to temporize too much when down fifteen–forty or love–forty. Maintain good pace. Excessive caution, a too-soft "push" shot is just as dumb as a wild, all-out gambling effort. Poise, keeping one's cool, is the court coverer's temperament.

One other point that the court coverer should remember is that the genius of tennis scoring is that it offers the chance of coming back from defeat, of actually losing more points and games than one's opponent, yet winning because the decisive factor in scoring is the set, the winner being the player who wins the majority of sets. For the court coverer, by definition a player who vows to hang in, this means you have the wonderful chance for resurrection no matter how many points and games you have lost in a bad set. Hang in—the tennis scoring is on your side!

This principle of maintaining pace—on serve, on ground shots, on volleys—applies equally to the climactic moments when your court coverage has finally reached pay dirt, when you are about to win your match. *Hit hard and firmly then*. Don't, as so many club players do, weaken in the clutch, playing too safely. That is an endemic shortcoming of the too-defensive court coverer. Once court coverage has brought you to the brink of victory, don't let its excess—that is, total reliance on just keeping the ball in play—nullify your attainment. Here is the time when hitting out with authority becomes the wisest *percentage* tennis.

VI

Angles and Depth; Stop and Go

The court coverer must, by definition, understand the variables in the "turf" he defends and the opponent's turf, which he is determined to exploit. First, to deal with defense of one's own turf, consider lateral coverage. Lateral coverage—moving from side to side, corner to corner—is, of course, as crucial to court coverage as the capacity to move up and back from baseline to net and back. And it poses a special difficulty to court coverage, but one that can be overcome if dealt with consciously. The difficulty is this: When the court coverer has to dig laterally to get to a tough shot, often he will err in his return, hitting short or actually netting the return. Why? Because he has not sufficiently compensated for the fact that *his body momentum is not supporting the shot*, is not behind the shot, but is directed offcourt. This means that one has to compensate by hitting harder and following through with an almost excessive stroke.

The truth of this is apparent as one confronts the opposite situation, with its opposite danger, namely, instead of moving laterally to get to a shot, running forward on a short shot, when your body momentum is behind your stroke. Here the court coverer's concern must be to avoid allowing that body momentum to add to the stroke itself and thus result in an overhit ball that zooms ("unaccount-

Running game though tennis is, you must be virtually stationary when actually making the shot, even following your serve
to the net—as you make that first volley, you "pause for station identification," as illustrated.

ably"; you stroked it softly, you thought) past the baseline.

An important footnote here: For court coverage, many
players, even good ones, fail to appreciate that, precisely
because of this factor of body momentum, one must *stop,
be stationary*, when actually making one's shot. This is a
book on court coverage, and I cannot overstate that, para-
dox though it may appear, while court coverage means
you must run *for* the shot, you set yourself firmly at the
moment you *make* the shot. This is eminently true, for instance, in what is considered a running maneuver—
namely, following one's serve to the net. Yes, serve, and
run in; but as you make that first volley, almost invariably
you "pause for station identification"—you halt as you actually make the volley (or half volley) going in. *Then*
proceed in to the net position.

Indeed, virtually the only shot hit deliberately on the
run (I say deliberately since one is necessarily on the run
and hits in desperation at a big offense shot that has you
straining just to keep alive) is the approach down the line
as you go in, the classic undercut or flat shot down the
line as you take over the offensive. Yes, on this shot you
are making it as you move in.

Covering the court has multiple meanings—covering in
the sense of defensive "territorial" coverage, and covering
in the subtler senses we have been analyzing that deal
with the psychology, tactical shots, etc., that a *court
coverer*, above all other players, must master. But covering the court also entails full exploitation of the court surface, especially knowledgeable exploitation of angles. Exploitation of angles is surprisingly neglected, even by
superior club players. This is so because, quite properly,

depth and *pace* are essential qualities in ground play and
are always first emphasized. But they must not be to the
neglect of angles.

For instance, the sharply angled *short* crosscourt to the
backhand (not the forehand) is a peculiarly effective and
underutilized shot. It is a shot the court coverer may use
in returns of service, but more particularly in rallies
against harder-hitting opponents. Here the court coverer
—in the sense of exploiting the full dimension of the court
—can break up his opponent's offense. The reasons are
these. The short—to the depth of the service line only—
crosscourt to the backhand will be a low shot scooting
wide past the alley. The opponent must play it with unusual care—if he tries a down-the-line shot, he confronts
the net at its highest point. Also, since it is on his backhand, he will probably be denied the luxury of driving it
back hard crosscourt because it requires a topspin to keep
the drive in court, and most opponents don't have a
topspin backhand drive capacity, only the standard undercut backhand. (They *will* have topspin on the
forehand, so beware hitting the same short, radically
angled shot to the forehand.)

Again, this short, sharply angled backhand shot, well ex-
ecuted, will simultaneously allow you, the court coverer,
to hit your *second* shot deep to the opponent's forehand
corner, after you have yanked him wide and short on his
backhand, disrupting his preferred rallying pattern. See
how often the very best of the senior tournament players
in the forty-five- and fifty-five-year-old categories (most
of them "court coverers") have mastered this use of the
short-angle shot.

There is a bonus in this short-angle-to-the-backhand-shot: It is potent against the two-handed backhand player, more and more of whom are developing due to the celebrity of such rising two-handed stars as Chris Evert, Jimmy Connors, and Bjorn Borg. The low, short, sharply angled backhand goes to their most vulnerable spot. Watch how their best opponents try to exploit that weakness. Two-handers have trouble bending to and stroking that particular shot.

Now, the court coverer must bear in mind, with respect to angles, that angles beget angles—that is, a sharply angled shot tends to invite the same shot in reprise. Be alert to that. And remember, too, it takes an angle to make an angle—that is, the court coverer's best opportunity for the sharp, short-angle shot is when he gets a shot that is wide and thus enables him to truly exploit the angle in return.

The court coverer above all others must appreciate that there is only one ultimate defense against attacking shots whose special demon is the sharpness of their angle so that one is pulled dangerously out of court. It is the lob. Pulling you way off court is a prime obective of the angle shot. Such shots can make life miserable for the court coverer because not only does being pulled out of court automatically mean the entire court is then opened up for a putaway shot, it also means much running and straining for the court coverer, who has, under the circumstances, to run over many many yards to sustain the ball in play, a tiring procedure. The defense, of course, is to lob. The court coverer must not hesitate or be ashamed to use the lob against sharp angles.

Pulled wide of the court and short, it is dangerous to try to hit to your opponent's near corner because the territory to hit is a small patch. And the net is high near the net post for a line shot, while a crosscourt is also dangerous, since a cutoff volley will catch you absolutely dead. So, court coverer that you are, lob—high, deep, defensively—to get yourself back into position. I am, of course, referring to an *in extremis* situation, a really tough shot, for if it isn't too tough, then, as noted above, by all means the court coverer should try to exploit the angle himself and hit at an extreme angle with maximum "mustard" on the shot to end the point. Easier said than done.

Indeed, this is axiomatic. Court coverage is an entire system of tennis, if you will, and is unthinkable without the use of the lob as the ultimate safety valve—not to be overdone, but always borne in mind, always the last arrow in the quiver, never unconsidered when the pressure is overwhelming.

VII

Court Coverage in Doubles

Doubles is "a whole 'nother game." Period. Yes and no. Virtually all that has been stated heretofore applies, but there are court-covering situations unique to doubles because one can hit certain shots confident that, if they don't become outright winners, their return can be handled by your partner.

Court coverage in doubles entails as a fundamental that you and your partner almost invariably must cover as a team in tandem so far as position goes, not one up, one back (except in serving), but generally as an attacking unit, striving to gain the net position. Unlike singles, doubles matches are always, or nearly always, won by the offensively superior team. That does not mean that percentage tennis, court-covering percentage tennis, is not important. Indeed it is. But the stress is on achieving the optimum finishing-point situations—that is, both at the net with your opponents on the defensive—because simply covering the backcourt will seldom prevail in any doubles beyond the lowest hacker level.

For a full comprehension of doubles tactics, do read Billy Talbert's classic *The Game of Doubles*. So far as court coverage per se is concerned, there are basics such as the tandem position noted above. One surprisingly often misplayed situation the court coverer should understand is the matter of coverage when you and your partner have extricated yourselves from a bad spot with a high, deep lob, forcing your opponents to retrieve. Follow in to the net, ready to pounce upon the likely desperate lob back; don't linger on the baseline—that isn't "covering the court," it is just missing an offensive opportunity.

Another key lesson in *doubles* coverage is generally to eschew the desperate shot down the line when you are forced wide or deep. Play percentages; hit low for the center, reducing your chance of outright error, and remembering that you *do* have a partner who can play the volley return while you have pulled yourself back into court.

A difficult but rewarding tactic in doubles court coverage is this situation: You are up, your partner back receiving in the ad court. He returns the serve, the server has moved in and makes a standard volley down the center. You are up and in the forehand side of the court, and in nine out of ten cases you will try to intercept the server's first volley, more often than not a tough, low volley or half volley on your backhand. The thing to do is have an understanding with your partner (who has just returned service from the left-hand court, remember) for him to take the shot *on his forehand* rather than you stabbing desperately at it with your backhand. He is farther back, has more time, and probably can take it on the bounce as a regular shot, not a tricky half volley. This situation is one of the most frequently botched plays in club-level tennis, but it is correctible for the good court coverer as explained.

Another principle in court coverage that is especially pertinent to doubles is this prime axiom: On hitting all balls within the service line-to-net area (that is, very

Here is a rewarding tactic in doubles court coverage. Server A has served to B (in ad court), and has followed his serve in and volleyed B's return of service down the center. Player C on the receiving team, up at the net, more often than not will try to intercept that server's first volley, a tough low volley or half volley on his backhand. But he should instead have an understanding with his partner B for B to take the shot *on his forehand* because he is farther back, has more time, and can probably take it on the bounce as a regular shot, not a tricky half volley. This situation is one of the most frequently botched plays in club tennis, but is correctible as explained.

short shots), *never temporize*; never try a delicate drop shot or a cautious slow shot, but instead *put mustard on the shot*, put it away. This is the court coverer's pay-dirt area, virtually the only situation when the *percentage* shot is the hardest possible putaway shot, because it is so safe and easy to do at the close-in range. The opposite tactic—to temporize when you're in killing area—is to invite disaster, since a heads-up doubles team will murder you by getting to, say, a drop shot, or easily passing you if you've hit a weak, tentative shot to them, while you are vulnerable close in to the net. Again, it is exasperating to observe how very often this situation is botched.

Indeed, failing to "put mustard" on the close-in shot is almost the most common and among the very dumbest mistakes of faulty court coverage in both singles and doubles. Why reach pay dirt with shrewd coverage only to nullify the advantage at the climax? To repeat, on balls inside the service line always put the mustard on, put them away.

With respect to doubles court coverage, it is very useful to appreciate two interconnected concepts: (1) cover all shots in your orbit and (2) learn the automatic move, what might be called the automatics of doubles coverage. What is meant here is that one player obviously must handle all shots in his reach, his domain. Now, this sounds self-evident, but in fact it is dismaying to see how often even a good club player will fail to go for shots (mostly volleys) that clearly come in his orbit, because he is not alert to the shot and because it involves a fast interception volley. To illustrate, the classic example here is when you are up at net, say on the forehand side, and your partner is back, forced deep off to the backhand corner. Your opponent or opponents hit a hard shot angled between you on an angle toward your forehand or deuce court. Now you are up at the net and the ball zooms over

One of the "automatics" of doubles coverage: You *must* cover
your orbit—for example, your opponents have somehow forced
your partner A deep off to the backhand corner, rushed the
net, and smacked your partner's return with a volley angled
to your deuce court. There is no way your partner can possibly get to the shot; it's in your orbit and is an "automatic"
—the only option is for you, B, to try to intercept the volley.
All too many club players watch that shot go by, on the timid
or mindless assumption that it's the backcourt man's shot. It
may indeed be a tough cutoff volley for you, but *this is an
automatic:* You have to take the shot.

the center of the net, angling by you to your corner.
There is no way your partner, who has been pulled wide
and deep on the backhand side, can get to that shot—it is
"in *your* orbit," if anyone's. Only you have a crack at it,
and, aware court coverer that you are, you dig for it. Dig

you must because *it is the only option.* Don't, as all too many club players do, watch it go by, on the timid and lazy mental assumption that it is your backcourt partner's shot. It may be a tough cutoff volley for you, but *this is an automatic:* You *have* to take the shot. There is no alternative. So the message here is be aware of, be ready for all such "automatics"—those shots necessarily in your orbit, and indeed outright winners for your opponents if you don't try to accomplish the automatic response.

As you and your partner play more together, you will gain a better understanding of your coverage strategies and should discuss all such "orbit" and "automatics" situations.

When playing doubles with a left-handed partner who normally (but not always) will play the ad court position, be sure to come to an understanding of handling down-the-center shots, since both of you will be taking them on your backhands. Let the man with the securer backhand, and especially the faster or longer-reach man, who can best "dig" center-court volleys out of the ground, generally cover the down-the-center shots.

One final tip on doubles for the court coverer, a tip that contradicts one of the clichés of many teachers. It is this: Don't be afraid to use the lob volley. It is not the excessively difficult shot that some pros allege. Indeed, it is surprisingly simple, surprisingly effective, and, in any event, essential in the arsenal of the court coverer. It can be a useful ploy in both singles and doubles but, because you are involved in head-to-head, both-at-the-net volleying duels most frequently in doubles, it is most used in doubles. When a volley is banged directly at you and it is unlikely (because of its angle, height, position, or whatever)

Don't be afraid to use the lob volley. When a volley is banged
directly at you (principally in head-to-head, both teams-at-
the-net volleying duels), simply block the shot defensively
with your racket head turned to an angle that will loft the
ball high and into deep court. It is a "percentage" shot, a
keep-the-ball-in-play tactic under severe pressure that is not
as excessively difficult as most players assume.

that you can make a putaway of it, then simply block it
with your racket head turned to an angle that will loft the
blocked ball over your opponents' heads to deep court. To
repeat, this sounds harder than it is to do—and the re-
wards for the court coverer (it is a percentage-shot, keep-
the-ball-in-play ploy) are immense. He has both played
the tactically safest coverage shot, yet may have the satis-
faction of converting a somewhat desperate situation into
a winning riposte.

VIII

Final Tips for the Court Coverer

There are many ancient saws for tennis players like "Keep your eye on the ball," "Don't change a winning game," etc., but two in particular are especially important to effective court coverage. One is don't change your mind about your shot. A high percentage of errors comes from last-second changes of mind, resulting in the tentative shot—the neither lob nor drive shot, the too timidly angled shot, the floater. Covering the court presumes a purposeful, comprehensive strategy of play *with the objective of being the last one to hit the ball safely in the rally.* That strategy can be disastrously affected by indecision and second-thought shotmaking. Indeed, second-thought shotmaking can even hurt your stroke production, since it leads to failure to follow through on the stroke, to pull-ups on the forehand and too short a shot in returning on the backhand. Be purposeful, poised, and definite in your shotmaking if you intend to be an effective court coverer.

A final tip on court coverage, and one that may seem contradictory to those who think of court coverage as defensive tennis—it isn't; it's percentage, "attrition" tennis—is to remember that the best defense is a strong offense. This old principle is subtle as well as sound. Steadiness in play, getting to every shot, is immeasurably enhanced by the court coverer's attitude on each shot. That means more than only getting to the ball. It means, too, an unrelenting effort to put the opponent on the defensive, to convert each rally, each shot into an advantageous position so that your "turf" is rendered as inviolable as possible and you are that less apt to make an error induced by your opponent's pressure. Strive for the offensive posture, not by mindless drives or smashes, but by the shot that, in the favorite words of the best of all American tennis writers, Allison Danzig, "elicits" an error. This may require depth, spin, angle, "mustard," a subtle lob or drop shot, whatever.

The nice irony is that this effort to place the opponent on the defensive, to seek on each shot to elicit an error, means purposeful, thoughtful, aggressive tennis, the crucial characteristics of superior court coverers. Indeed, the very adoption of this attitude creates the kind of mental concentration decisive for superior court coverage. As I said at the outset, covering the court well is more an act of the mind and will than sheer physical prowess in running down the shot. The mind and the will are the ultimate keys to covering the court.

With the co-operation of the United States Tennis Association, Doubleday has published the following titles in this series:

SPEED, STRENGTH, AND STAMINA: CONDITIONING FOR TENNIS, by Connie Haynes with Eve Kraft and John Conroy
Detailed descriptions of exercises for tennis players, and suggestions for keeping in shape.

TACTICS IN WOMEN'S SINGLES, DOUBLES, AND MIXED DOUBLES, by Rex Lardner
A book for women tennis players, with specific suggestions for taking advantage of opponents' weaknesses.

SINISTER TENNIS, by Peter Schwed
How to play against left-handers, and also with left-handers as doubles partners.

RETURNING THE SERVE INTELLIGENTLY, by Sterling Lord
How you can reduce errors, minimize the server's advantage, and launch your own attack.

COVERING THE COURT, by Edward T. Chase
How to be a winning court coverer and keep maximum pressure on your opponent.

FINDING AND EXPLOITING YOUR OPPONENT'S WEAKNESSES, by Rex Lardner

THE SERVE AND THE OVERHEAD SMASH, by Peter Schwed
How the intermediate player can best hit the big shots.

The following titles are in preparation:
THE HALF VOLLEY AND THE VOLLEY
GROUND STROKES
THE TENNIS PLAYER'S DIET AND FITNESS BOOK
SPECIALIZATION IN SINGLES, DOUBLES, AND MIXED DOUBLES
USTA COACHES' FAVORITE DRILLS

R